SPORTS ALL-STARS

NEYMAR

Jon M. Fishman

Lerner Publications • Minneapolis

Lerner Publications Company
A division of Lerner Publishing Group, Inc.
241 First Avenue North
Minneapolis, MN 55401 USA

For reading levels and more information, look up this title at www.lernerbooks.com.

Main body text set in Albany Std 15/22. Typeface provided by Agfa.

Library of Congress Cataloging-in-Publication Data

Names: Fishman, Jon M., author.
Title: Neymar / Jon M. Fishman.
Description: Minneapolis : Lerner Publications, [2018] | Series: Sports All-Stars |
    Includes bibliographical references and index. | Audience: Ages: 7–11. | Audience:
    Grades: 4 to 6.
Identifiers: LCCN 2018006171 (print) | LCCN 2018004402 (ebook) |
    ISBN 9781541524675 (eb pdf) | ISBN 9781541524590 (library binding : alk.
    paper) | ISBN 9781541528055 (paperback: alk. paper)
Subjects: LCSH: Neymar, 1992—Juvenile literature. | Soccer players—Brazil—
    Biography—Juvenile literature. | Paris-Saint-Germain-Football-Club—History—
    Juvenile literature.
Classification: LCC GV942.7.N455 (print) | LCC GV942.7.N455 F57 2018 (ebook) |
    DDC 796.334092 [B]—dc23

LC record available at https://lccn.loc.gov/2018006171

Manufactured in the United States of America
1 - 44535 - 34785 - 4/25/2018

CONTENTS

FRANCE

Neymar winds up to kick the ball during a game against Stade Rennais.

Neymar and his Paris Saint-Germain (PSG) teammates had the ball deep in the Stade Rennais end of the soccer field. Stade Rennais couldn't keep up with PSG's short, quick passes. Suddenly, Neymar was open in front of the goal. He stepped forward and blasted a shot high into the net. The score gave PSG a 2–0 lead.

It was January 7, 2018, and the two teams were facing off in the **Coupe de France**. The loser would be out of the tournament. But PSG expected to win. They had won the Coupe de France championship three years in a row.

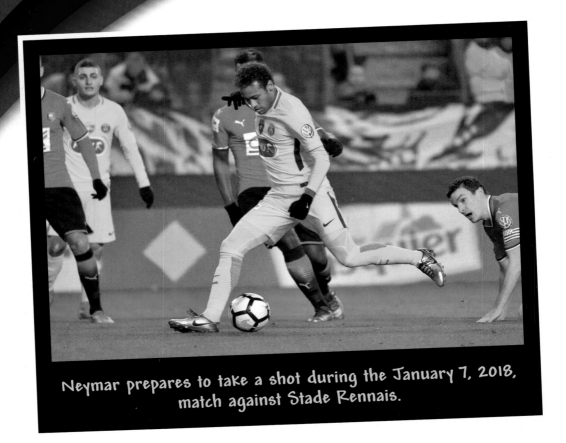

Neymar prepares to take a shot during the January 7, 2018, match against Stade Rennais.

Angel di Maria knocked in a short shot for PSG to make the score 3–0. Then Neymar struck again in the 43rd minute of the match. It started with di Maria. He passed the ball across the field to Kylian Mbappe. Mbappe was open to shoot, but he had an even better option. He passed the ball to the front of the goal where Neymar waited. The PSG **forward** swung his leg at the rolling ball and sent it streaking into the goal. That made the score 4–0. The game ended with a PSG win, 6–1.

Neymar was in his first season with PSG. The team was one of the best in Europe before he joined them. With Neymar, the team seemed unbeatable. "He is an exceptional player and he helps us plenty,"

Neymar (right) celebrates a goal with teammate Kylian Mbappe.

goalkeeper Kevin Trapp said. Neymar and PSG had a shot at the team's fourth straight Coupe de France.

Brazilian soccer players have a long history of using just one name. Pele is the most famous one-named star from Brazil. He helped Brazil win the World Cup three times: 1958, 1962, and 1970.

Neymar takes to the field in Brazil in 2010.

Neymar da Silva Santos Jr. was born on February 5, 1992, in Sao Paulo, Brazil. His father, Neymar Sr., played **pro** soccer. Neymar fell in love with the sport before he was three years old.

Neymar (center) walks with his family and a close friend, Jo Amancio (left), after Neymar joined PSG in 2017.

Neymar Sr.'s soccer career ended soon after his son was born. He began working three jobs to support the family. Neymar, his parents, and his little sister, Rafaella, all lived with Neymar's grandparents. The family of four shared a room in the house. Sometimes there wasn't enough money for electricity. They spent those nights by candlelight.

Neymar played soccer after school. "As soon as I arrived home I used to grab my [ball] and go straight out and I'd play until late at night with my friends," he said.

They also played *futsal*. This sport is similar to soccer. Usually, *futsal* is played indoors with five players on each side. The ball is smaller than a soccer ball.

Neymar shined on the soccer field and the *futsal* court. He moved with grace and **agility** that other players couldn't match. He joined Santos Futebol Clube (FC) in Sao Paulo when he was 11 years old. Neymar played soccer for Santos FC's youth teams. He trained and learned about the sport. Neymar was ready for Santos FC's top team by 2009. In 2010, he scored five goals in one game!

Neymar (center) celebrates with two Santos FC teammates during a game in 2009.

Neymar poses with his Puskas Award, the award given for the best goal of the year.

In a match in 2011, Neymar passed the ball and then streaked toward the goal. A teammate passed it right back to Neymar. Four defenders surrounded him. Suddenly, he kicked the ball between his legs and poked it past the defender in front of him. He was open and kicked the ball into the net. The amazing move won a prize as the best goal in the world in 2011.

Neymar became a member of FC Barcelona in 2013.

By 2013, soccer fans everywhere knew about Neymar. His flashy goals and big smile made him popular. He felt ready to move on from Brazil. Some of the world's most successful teams wanted Neymar to join them. He chose FC Barcelona in Spain. "I had a lot of offers but I followed my heart," he said. He followed the money too. Barcelona agreed to pay Neymar millions of dollars. The team also paid millions of dollars to Neymar's parents. The family's days of worrying about money were over.

Neymar's parents didn't push him to play soccer. He enjoyed the sport, but he wasn't sure he wanted to be a soccer player when he grew up. He dreamed of becoming Superman or a Power Ranger.

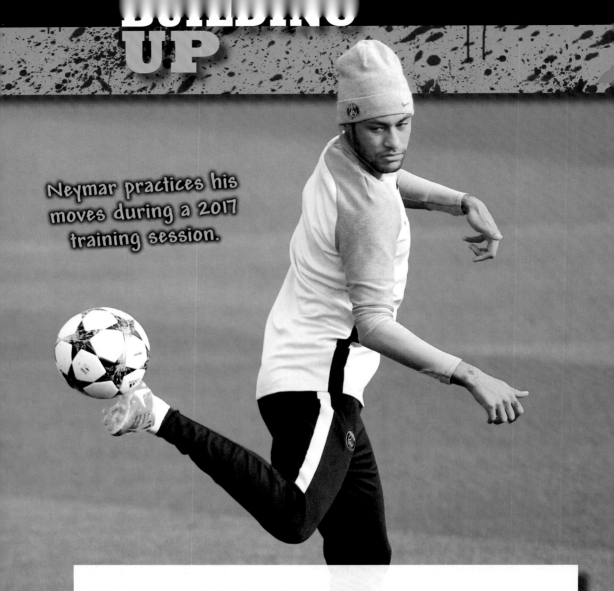

Neymar practices his moves during a 2017 training session.

Neymar thinks fast and moves even faster. He gives *futsal* some of the credit for his soccer skills. A *futsal* match is nonstop action. The court is much smaller than a soccer field. Players

Neymar (center) practices with his PSG teammates in 2017.

learn to control the ball in tight spaces and make quick decisions. Mastering the court as a kid made Neymar more confident on the soccer field.

He continues to sharpen his skills as a pro soccer player. PSG practices are tough and intense. Players rush through fast-paced exercises that test their passing and shooting skills. Practices also provide plenty of chances to have fun. Neymar jokes with teammates, juggles the ball, and does tricks.

Neymar had the talent of a superstar when he moved to Spain in 2013. Yet he was smaller than most pro soccer players. He weighed about 130 pounds (59 kg). Neymar worked hard to gain weight and improve his strength.

Soccer practice is usually early in the morning. Then Neymar heads to the gym after lunch. Lifting weights builds up his muscles and helps prevent injuries. He

Neymar completes a training drill while playing for Barcelona in 2015.

Neymar (left) and his teammates warm up before a PSG practice in 2017.

also does **cardio** work. Exercises such as running and swimming strengthen his heart and lungs.

After practice and exercise, Neymar spends time with **physical therapists**. They stretch and rub his muscles and teach Neymar how to care for his body. Physical therapy helps athletes heal from injuries and recover after long workouts. PSG hired two physical therapists just to work with Neymar.

It takes a lot of food to fuel Neymar's athletic life. As a kid, he ate whatever he wanted, including lots of sugar. But he follows a more healthful diet as a pro soccer star. Salads, beans, and rice are on his daily menu. To increase his weight, he eats high-**calorie** foods such as pasta and burgers. Special drinks with lots of calories help Neymar stay in shape.

Neymar runs to prepare for a game.

Do you want to work out with Neymar? Nabufit is an app that helps people exercise. It has advice and examples from Neymar and other superstar athletes.

FLYING HIGH

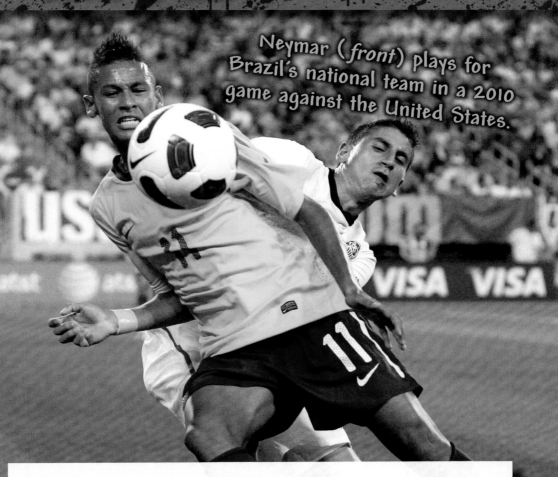

Neymar (front) plays for Brazil's national team in a 2010 game against the United States.

When does a star athlete become a superstar? For Neymar, it may have been in 2010 when he joined Brazil's national team. His wild hairstyle got almost as much attention from Brazilian fans as his fast feet.

A few years later, Neymar became an international megastar when he moved from Brazil to play for FC Barcelona. He also became rich, and he likes to have fun with his money. Neymar once arrived to soccer practice in a helicopter. He drives expensive cars and flies on private jets. His famous friends include musicians Justin Bieber and Drake.

Neymar arrives at a 2018 event in London, England, in an orange sports car.

Other times, Neymar likes to hang out at home. He's close with his family—especially his sister, Rafaella. In 2017, Neymar and Rafaella dressed up together for Halloween. He wore a Joker costume, and she dressed as Catwoman.

Neymar hasn't forgotten his childhood and his family's struggle to survive. He helps people around the world with his money and time. The Neymar Jr. Project Institute in Brazil has a swimming pool, classrooms, and much more. The institute instructs kids in sports and schoolwork. "It makes me really happy to do something for these kids and their families," Neymar said.

Neymar's sister, Rafaella, attends an event in Sao Paulo in 2017.

Neymar (*second from right*) poses with children and other professional athletes during an event hosted by the Neymar Jr. Project Institute.

Another project Neymar is involved with helps provide clean water to people in Brazil. He worked with FC Barcelona to spread sports among young people in South America. And sometimes Neymar gives back by simply visiting a young fan.

Neymar hosts a special yearly competition at the Neymar Jr.'s Project Institute. Neymar Jr.'s Five is a tournament for teams of five to seven soccer players. They play on a small field with no goalkeepers. Each time a team scores, a player on the other team must leave the field. A match ends when one team runs out of players.

Teams represent their home countries at Neymar Jr.'s Five. 2018, more than 100,000 players took part in the tournament. They came from more than 60 countries around the world.

Neymar plays a game in the Neymar Jr.'s Five tournament in 2016.

Neymar (left) celebrates with his FC Barcelona teammates during a 2016 game.

Neymar enjoyed incredible success with FC Barcelona. He played alongside Lionel Messi, whom many fans consider the world's best player. By the 2014–2015 season, Neymar trailed only Messi in scoring for Barcelona. The team won the

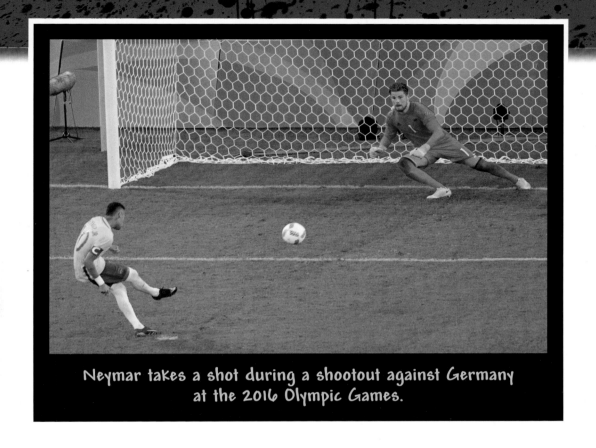

Neymar takes a shot during a shootout against Germany at the 2016 Olympic Games.

Champions League that year. Neymar had 10 goals in the tournament.

The 2016 Olympic Games took place in Rio de Janeiro, Brazil. With the local fans behind them, Brazil's national team made it to the final match. Neymar scored on a **free kick**, and Brazil went on to beat Germany to win the gold medal. "This is one of the best things that has happened in my life," he said.

In 2017, rumors swirled among fans that Neymar would change teams. The rumors became reality when PSG paid FC Barcelona more than $260 million for Neymar. PSG also agreed to pay him more than $50 million each season. That made Neymar the best-paid soccer player in the world.

Fans wondered why Neymar left FC Barcelona. He said it wasn't for the money. He was just ready for new challenges. But rumors about Neymar's future didn't stop in 2018. News reports said soccer powerhouse Real Madrid might offer PSG even more money for Neymar. No matter where Neymar plays, he'll thrill fans with his incredible goals and smooth moves.

Neymar greets his fans after joining PSG in 2017.

Neymar plays for PSG in a 2018 match against Real Madrid.

All-Star Stats

Some of soccer's biggest stars have played for Brazil's national soccer team. Neymar already ranks highly on the team's all-time scoring list. He could play for the team for years to come. Do you think someday he could be number one?

Most Goals Scored in Brazil National Team History

Player	Goals
Pele	77
Ronaldo	62
Romario	55
Neymar	50
Zico	48
Bebeto	39
Rivaldo	35
Jairzinho	33
Ronaldinho	33
Ademir	32
Tostao	32

Source Notes

7   Jonathan Johnson, "Paris Saint-Germain 'Returned in Style' in Coupe de France Win—Emery," *ESPN*, January 7, 2018, http://www.espn.com/soccer/paris -saint-germain/story/3340796/paris-saint-germain -returned-in-style-in-coupe-de-france-win-vs-rennes -emery.

9   "Neymar Opens Up on Learning New Tricks from Futsal and Street Soccer," *Barcelona Live*, accessed January 11, 2018, https://tribuna.com/fcbarcelona/en /news/1684001.

13   "Neymar: Barcelona Complete £49m Signing of Brazilian Striker," *BBC*, June 3, 2013, http://www.bbc .com/sport/football/22760770.

21   Dermot Corrigan, "Neymar Uses Charity as Motivation to Win More Trophies for Barcelona," *ESPN*, March 8, 2016, http://www.espn.com/soccer /barcelona/story/2824614/neymar-uses-charity-work -as-motivation-to-win-more-trophies.

25   Michael Emons, "Rio Olympics 2016: Brazil Beat Germany on Penalties to Win Men's Football Gold," *BBC*, August 21, 2016, http://www.bbc.com/sport /olympics/36691461.

Glossary

agility: ability to move quickly and smoothly

calorie: a unit of energy in food

cardio: a type of workout designed to get the heart pumping and improve blood flow

Champions League: a yearly tournament featuring Europe's top soccer teams

Coupe de France: a yearly tournament featuring France's top soccer teams

forward: a player whose main job is to score goals

free kick: a kick awarded to a team after the other team has committed a foul

physical therapists: people who help athletes and others recover from and prevent injuries

pro: something done for money that many people do for fun

World Cup: a tournament held every four years featuring the world's top soccer teams

Further Information

Neymar
http://www.neymaroficial.com/en

Neymar Jr.'s Five
https://www.neymarjrsfive.com/en

Paris Saint-Germain
https://en.psg.fr

Savage, Jeff. *FC Barcelona: Soccer Champions*. Minneapolis: Lerner Publications, 2019.

Savage, Jeff. *Soccer Super Stats*. Minneapolis: Lerner Publications, 2018.

Torres, John Albert. *Neymar: Champion Soccer Star*. New York: Enslow, 2018.

Index

Photo Acknowledgments

Image credits: Nick Potts/PA Images/Getty Images, p. 2 (background); JEAN-SEBASTIEN EVRARD/AFP/Getty Images, pp. 4–5; LOIC VENANCE/AFP/Getty Images, pp. 6, 7; MAURICIO LIMA/AFP/Getty Images, p. 8; Jean Catuffe/Getty Images, p. 9; BRUNO DOMINGOS/REUTERS/Newscom, p. 10; Stuart Franklin/FIFA/Getty Images, p. 11; David Ramos/Getty Images, p. 12; FRANCK FIFE/AFP/Getty Images, pp. 14, 18; KARIM JAAFAR/AFP/Getty Images, p. 15; Mike Hewitt/FIFA/Getty Images, p. 16; Aurelien Meunier/Getty Images, p. 17; Andy Mead/Icon Sports Wire/Getty Images, p. 19; Matt Crossick/ZUMA Press/Newscom, p. 20; EDUARDO MARTINS/Brazil Photo Press/Alamy Live News, p. 21; Miguel Schincariol/AFP/Getty Images, p. 22; Samo Vidic/Getty Images, p. 23; NurPhoto//Getty Images, p. 24; JOHANNES EISELE/AFP/Getty Images, p. 25; Dave Winter/Icon Sport/Getty Images, p. 26; VI-Images/Getty Images, p. 27.

Cover: Nick Potts/PA Images/Getty Images.